Also by Lucia Perillo

Luck Is Luck

Luck Is Luck

POEMS

Lucia Perillo

RANDOM HOUSE

NEW YORK

Published in the United States by Random House, an imprint of The
Random House Publishing Group, a division of Random House, Inc.,
New York.

RANDOM HOUSE and colophon are registered trademarks of Random
House, Inc.

Library of Congress Cataloging-in-Publication Data

Perillo, Lucia Maria
    Luck is luck: poems / Lucia Perillo.—1st ed.
        p. cm.
    ISBN 1-4000-6323-X (alk. paper)
        I. Title.

    PS3566.E69146L83 2005
    811'.54—dc22   2004051084

Random House website address: www.atrandom.com

Printed in the United States of America on acid-free paper

9 8 7 6 5 4 3 2

Book design by Simon M. Sullivan

For my father

Contents

III

I

———————

Christ died for us, Paul taught? How strange
A god should think a man's requirements so
Excessive.

—Vassar Miller

To My Big Nose

Hard to believe there were actual years
when I planned to have you cut from my face—
hard to imagine what the world would have looked like
if not seen through your pink shadow.
You who are built from random parts
like a mythical creature—a gryphon or sphinx—
with the cartilage ball attached to your tip
and the plaque where the bone flares at the bridge
like a snake who has swallowed a small coin.
Seabird beak or tanker prow
with Modigliani nostrils, like those strolled out
from the dank studio and its close air,
with a *swish-swish* whisper from the nude's silk robe
as it parts and then falls shut again.
Then you're out on the sidewalk of Montparnasse
with its fumes of tulips and clotted cream
and clotted lungs and cigars and sewers—
even fumes from the lobster who walks on a leash.
And did his owner march slowly
or drag his swimmerets briskly along
through the one man's Parisian dogturd that is
the other man's cutting-edge conceptual art?
So long twentieth century, my Pygmalion.
So long rhinoplasty and the tummy tuck.
Let the vowels squeak through my sinus-vault.
like wet sheets hauled on a laundry line's rusty wheels.
Oh I am not so dumb as people have made me out,
what with your detours when I speak,
and you are not so cruel, though you frightened men off

all those years when I thought I was running the show,
pale ghost who has led me like a knife
continually slicing the future stepped into,
oh rudder/wing flap/daggerboard, my whole life
turning me this way and that.

Languedoc

Southern France, the troubadour age:
all these men running around in frilly sleeves.
Each is looking for a woman he could write a song about—
or the moonlight a woman, the red wine a woman,
there is even a woman called the Albigensian Crusade.
It's the tail end of the Dark Age
but if we wait a little longer it'll be the Renaissance
and the forms of the songs will be named and writ down;
wait: here comes the villanelle, whistling along the pike,
repeating the same words over and over
until I'm afraid my patience with your serenade
runs out: time's up. Long ago
I might have been attracted by your tights and pantaloons,
but now they just look silly, ditto for your instrument
that looks like a gourd with strings attached
(the problem is always the strings attached).
Langue d'oc, meaning the language of yes, as in
"Do you love me?" *Oc.* "Even when compared
to her who sports the nipple ring?" *Oc oc.*
"Will we age gracefully and die appealing deaths?"
Oc oc oc oc.
So much affirmation ends up sounding like
a murder of crows passing overhead
and it is easy to be afraid of murder-by-crow—
though sometimes you have to start flapping your arms
and follow them. And fly to somewhere the signs say:
Yes Trespassing, Yes Smoking,
Yes Alcohol Allowed on Premises, Yes Shirt Yes Shoes
Yes Service Yes. Yes Loitering
here by this rocky coast whose waves are small

and will not break your neck; this ain't no ocean, baby,
this is just the sea. Yes Swimming
Yes Bicycles Yes to Nude Sunbathing All Around,
Yes to Herniated Bathing-cappèd Veterans of World War One
and Yes to Leathery Old Lady Joggers.
Yes to their sun visors and varicose veins in back of their knees,
I guess James Joyce did get here first—
sometimes the Europeans seem much more advanced.
But you can't go through life regretting what you are,
yes, I'm talking to you in the baseball cap,
I'm singing this country-western song that goes: Yeah!
Oc! Yes! Oui! We!—will dive—right—in.

Christmas at Forty

Everyone needs a bosom for a pillow

Lying on the couch, staring up at the tree,
listening to that Indian raga trip-hop music
that one minute sounds like panpipes from Kashmir
and the next like a knife stuck into the speakers;
whammo! it hits: how unexpected life is.
One minute you're a punk driving around
in Eddie Butterford's blue Dodge, hashing
out the script for whatever happens next,
something that with any luck'll be
hallucinogenic . . . but then somehow you end up
with a whole mortgageful of ornaments in the attic
and even a green metal stand to triangulate the trunk.
And all you remember coming in between is a whole
lot of dithering about what to play
on the tape deck next—what was all the worry?
Now, in the pantry, you've got bottles
of liqueurs made by obscure sects of Italian monks;
in the bathroom all the vials bequeathed by your beloved
dying friends, who said, *Here, take the Demerol*
for a rainy day; take the Darvocet, you never know
when you might need it. Back in Eddie's car
nobody thought death would be the dealer
who someday would drop his manna on us
& if anyone had told me about these snowmen
made from crochet pom-pom balls
I would have said, *What are you, nuts?*
Sometimes in those days I panhandled
just to feel what it felt like to say, *Can I have*

a quarter, please? and then to cower in the brimstone
I thought for sure would rain down on my head.
But people just gave me more money than I asked for
and told me to go on home, so okay:
now I'm home. Where I've got not just the snowmen
and the tree stand, but also a glass angel for the top—
take that, all you sanctimonious quarter-givers.
No rainy days yet, but in just a minute
I'll take off my clothes and stomp around
with that strange guy who lives here.
After we drink to the health of the baby Jesus
with that very old brandy made from secret herbs.

Fizz Ed

Hard to pinpoint when the body starts turning.
One minute we're Burt Lancaster and Deborah Kerr
heavy-petting in the surf, but then the surf pulls out
sizzling like grease and suddenly we find
ourselves no longer shrouded
by the Pacific Ocean's glamorous foam.

Instead, think elephant seals: all snout and lobe and whisker.
All gluey effluence and ectomorphic musk.
So life heavily petted was not the real goods,
it was just a decoy good—that diverted us
for a season. Before the siege of flatulence
and the strange not-moles that multiply on the neck.

And where was the warning—about how the nose
would come to claim more real estate on the head?
How the bristles multiply in all its openings:
the nostrils' black forest, the white shrub in each ear?
No matter now, the birds and bees,
but I could have used a little heads-up about the eyebrows

(their mysterious length, their magisterial spread—)
if only to prepare me for this ancient Eastern European poet
speaking through the curved clear wall of my TV.
When his brow dips, the gray curls brush his cheeks
and I'm thinking, *Man oh man*—
pretty soon even the giants among us will take wing.

The Crows Start Demanding Royalties

Of all the birds, they are the ones
who mind their being armless most:
witness how, when they walk, their heads jerk
back and forth like rifle bolts.
How they heave their shoulders into each stride
as if they hoped that by some chance
new bones there would come popping out
with a boxing glove on the end of each.

Little Elvises, the hairdo slicked
with too much grease, they convene on my lawn
to strategize for their class-action suit.
Flight they would trade in a New York minute
for a black muscle car and a fist on the shift
at any stale green light. But here in my yard
by the Jack-in-the-Box Dumpster
they can only fossick in the grass for remnants

of the world's stale buns. And this
despite all the crow poems that have been written
because men like to see themselves as crows
(the head-jerk performed in the rearview mirror,
the dark brow commanding the rainy weather).
So I think I know how they must feel:
ripped off, shook down, taken to the cleaners.
What they'd like to do now is smash a phone against a wall.
But they can't, so each one flies to a bare branch and screams.

On the Destruction of the Mir

Every night space junk falls from the sky—
usually a titanium fuel tank. Usually falling
into the ocean, or into nowhere in particular
because ours is a planet of great vacancies,
no matter how much fog would be required
in downtown Tokyo. In the Skylab days
you'd see people on the streets wearing iron
helmets, like centurions. But nowadays
we go bareheaded, as if to say to the heavens:
Wake me when I am someone else.
Like the man whose car made fast acquaintance
with what Yeats would have called the bole of a tree.
And who now believes he has written
many of the latest hits, which he will sing
for you while he splits a cord of wood:
like a virgin—*whap!*—like a virgin—*whap!*—
until he's got enough fuel for the winter
and a million dollars stashed in an offshore bank.
You may think it's tragic, like my Buddhist friend
who claims that any existence means suffering,
though my gay friend says, *Phooey, what about*
Oscar night, what about making popcorn
and wrapping up with your sweetie
in that afghan your great-aunt made so long ago?
You don't have to dwell on the fact that she's dead
or bring up her last unkempt year in the home,
when she'd ask anyone who walked in the door
to give her a good clunk on the head. Instead,
what about her crocheting these squares
in preposterous colors, orange and green,

though why must their clashing be brought to the fore
if the yarn was enough to keep her happy?
In fact, don't the clashes light the sparks
in this otherwise corny thing? Which is safer
to make than a hole in the skull to let out
the off-gassing of one's bad spirits.
As in trepanation performed by the Incas,
who traded their melancholy for a helmet
made from a turtle shell. You never know
when your brain will require such armor—
could happen sometime when you least expect.
Could even happen when you are parked
behind your desk, where a very loud thump
makes you look up to discover a robin
diving into the window again and again.
It is spring, after all, and in its reflection
the bird may have found the perfect mate:
thus doth desire propel us headlong
toward the smash. Don't even try
translating glass into bird-speak; it only knows
it wants the one who dropped from sight.
Same one who beaned it, same one who's perched,
glaring back from a bough of the Japanese maple
with its breast fit to burst. And behind the lace
of new leaves, there's a wallpaper of clouds—
weighing hundreds of tons
but which float nonetheless—
in the blue sky that seemed to fit so well
when we first strapped it on our heads.

Le Deuxième Sexe

The famous Polish poet calls Simone de Beauvoir a Nazi hag
but to me she will always be her famous book,
the one with the Matisse paper cut on the cover,
a sad blue nude I took into the woods.
Where we college girls went to coax the big picture
from her, as if she could tell us how to use
all the strange blades on our Swiss army knives—
the firewood we arranged in either log cabin or tipi,
a little house built to be burned down.
Which could be a metaphor:
Simone as the wind puffing the damp flames,
a cloud with a mouth that became obsolete
once we started using gasoline. Still,
she gave me one lesson that sticks, which is:
do not take a paperback camping in the rain
or it may swell to many times its original size,
and if you start with a big book you'll end up
with a cinder block. In that vein I pictured Simone as huge
until (much later) I read that her size was near-midget—
imagine, if we took Gertrude Stein, we'd be there still,
trying to build some kind of travois to drag her body out.
The other thing I remember: a word, *immanence*—
meaning, you get stuck with the cooking and laundry
while the man gets to hit on all your friends in Paris.
Sure you can put the wet book in the oven
and try baking it like a cake. But the seam will stay soggy
even when the pages rise, ruffled like French pastry.
As far as laundry goes, it's best I steer clear,
what with my tendency to forget the tissues
wadded in my sleeves. What happens is

I think I'm being so careful, and everything
still comes out like the clearing where we woke.
Covered in flakes that were then the real thing:
snow. Which sounds more la-di-da in French.
But then the sun came up and all *la neige* vanished
like those chapters we grew bored with and had skipped.

The Lord's Prayer

This is what you remember: not the words
so much as the avalanche they made being said,
how it came or not at all in one rush, one breath,
like a cart lashed to many horses. How the simple
father handed off to a chain of bewilderments
like *daily bread,* like *hollow*
and *kingdom,* imported for what reason
from a different kind of story, the kind with a troll
and horses that lift each foot in turn like a girl's
bent wrist. *Trespass* was a sign nailed to a tree,
meaning you couldn't go any farther, which was why
the lady squatted here to cough out her child,
a story laced inside this one
but more secret. Having to do with
where the baby came from. Having to do
with the father's name. And long before
you saw the words written or knew much more
than that the black scratches like ants
papered everywhere in human places
were a way of making sound without sound,
the priest's call-and-response lured you here
to the grove of this secret, the father's
secret, which you could neither remember at first
nor stop the *whoosh* of its falling, once it came
in words so hard so furious in their quiet
that to this day you can't even think
your way through them without moving your lips.

The Believer

Bobby pins made the signs of the cross,
curling the dark hair at her temples: three
would go back to their cardboard sleeve, while the last
fixed the scrap of black lace to her head.
Black lace like the bra ads that came on Sundays
when the newspaper swelled: black lace like the struts
in a damselfly wing: black lace like the wilderness
with a formal structure at its core, formality
being one way women rested. On goes the lace,
and suddenly my mother's housework ceased.

And I never heard her speak of Jesus.
Such a nice boy was what she uttered wistfully
when even a grown man drowned in the river.

For mass she drove the Cadillac, steeling herself
to master its wheel, the kind of car
we'd take to heaven because its chrome
would suit the brightness there. We chose a pew
midway back where we did not sing loudly
and did not stay mute . . . but muttered, which struck us
as grace's median. Afterward we left
without pausing for the greeting and consolation that reigned
out on the steps, though on the way home
she'd stop at the deli for roast beef
that Mr. Albanese sliced for her from the rare, pink heart.

Hail Mary

The worst of it was the *fruit of thy womb* business,
through which the boys muddled in pig-latin sniggers
but being a girl you thought of plums, then grapefruit,
a catalog whose offerings led incrementally
to the one in school who'd gotten breasts,
her mother alky and her dad a pencil mark rubbed out.
After the bell rang she bundled her sadness
and walked it home in her serious coat,
the kind of girl who carried an umbrella, whose socks
defied the gravitational tug. And if other prayers
had someone offstage rumbling sheet metal, this one
made the *woof* of a broom swatting a rug,
a rhythmic thump below the scream
of the laundry tree she sent off on its wheel
around the backyard like a minor angel
flapping underpant-and-towel wings.
Someday she'd get pregnant by the shy and not-
unhandsome captain of the varsity baseball team
without even getting a bad rep; everyone knew
they'd marry quick and he'd die slow
from all those years of Red Man packed behind his lip.
But she wouldn't have loved him if there wasn't something
about him to work on; you know the type:
you loved her, you hated her
for ruling your life as the penmanship queen,
and you wanted to be her friend except you knew
beside her you'd be dirt. As far as Hailing Mary,
all you wanted to do was get through its last word,
though everyone knew this *death* was second-rate.
A man-god could get you bread or heaven, but pray
to a woman and all you got was prayed for in return.

The Floating Rib

Because a woman had eaten something
when a man told her not to. Because the man
who told her not to had made her
from another man's bone. That's why
men badgered the heart side of her chest,
knowing she could not give the bone back, knowing
she would always owe them that one bone.

And you could see how older girls who knew
their catechism armed themselves against it:
with the pike end of teasing combs
scabbarded in pocketbooks that clashed
against the regulation jumper's night-watch plaid.
In the girls' bathroom mirror, you watched them
hazard the spike at the edge of their eyes,

shepherding bangs through which they peered
like cheetahs in an upside-downward growing grass.
Then they'd mouth the words to "Runaway"
and run white lipstick around their lips—
white to announce they had no blood
so any wound would leave no trace, as Eve's
having nothing more to lose must have made her

fearless. What was weird was how soon
the ordinary days started running past them
like a river, and how willingly they entered it
and how they rose up on the other side. Tamed,
or—God, no—your *mother:* ready to settle
with whoever found the bone under her blouse
and give it over, and make a life out of getting it back.

Original Sin

When first they told me the serpent *beguiled* her
I pictured her eyes knocked loose and rattling round
like the gizmo you'd take with you into the closet
and pump with your thumb to make red and blue sparks.
You needed the darkness. You needed the quiet.
You needed the whisper of sleeves on your cheeks.
Most, you needed the shelf where your father's brown hats
squatted like toads, forget about sparks—
the mouth, not the eye, is the holy portal.
Hats with cool satin bellies and stained satin bands
that I put to my tongue when alone in their dark,
compelled by the mystery of his old sweat.
And this much I knew: such an outlaw rite
would command adult fury in the open. You could not
speak of sucking the hats' bowls to your face,
or of licking the grosgrain of their sweat-darkened ribbons:
there was no way to explain why you even wanted this.
Let them think I was in there fooling with my Black Cat sparker
and not tasting the wax that came out of his ears,
not hungry for everything about him that was forbidden.
God cursed the snake—*Thou shalt eat nothing but dust*—
but wasn't Snake a scapegoat for the wrong
that God himself had done? To name
out of all paradise the one thing denied her,
so Eve would spend those first days walking round
with *apple apple* filling hours in her head?
Sour, sweet—how it tasted went unsaid. Either way,
I doubt the fruit lived up to what she would expect.

New Hat

Because God did not want to look down from his going up
and see the tops of female heads—go figure—
come every Easter my sister and I wore hats
instead of our normal bobby-pinned mantillas.
We liked the snakeskin of our faces
in the speckled shadows of their brims,
which we *felt* we could feel, this darker light
falling in a misshaped wheel that the whole body
crowded into. One year it was a blue boater
from which a daisy telescoped like an antenna,
another year a bonnet with raffia birds
stitched to its crown. My mother took us
all the way down to Yonkers to pick them out
. . . at Klein's, with its bins of tangled goods
over which the women clawed like lions
taking down a springbok. And to this day
my sister is angry about those cheap Klein's hats,
those hats she says were as rickety
as the boat sheds by the river.
If she's right, I can't tell; I try putting myself
back in the pew, under the new weight
of my skull while my eyeballs scroll up.
Maybe the daisy swaggering there on its stalk
did make me look like an idiot, so close
did the damfool trail behind the latest chic.
But God wouldn't care, he was busy dying;
he was going up. Where all he'd see of me
was a blue straw disk, and not my eyes
rolled like a zombie's in the shade of my hat,

or the place underchin where the cheap Klein's elastic
was making a red line that would still be there
later, when God turned away from our unbridled heads.

The Cardinal's Nephews

They started out like the rest of us, huns
of the vacant fields behind the houses,
where our arrows punctured ancient mattresses
that wobbled drunkenly among the asters.
It wounded me to think about the cardinal's brother
fornicating even once for each of all his sons,
but when they tied me in the staghorns
and ran their Matchbox cars over my feet, suddenly
it was me too swooning with that fervor to breed an empire.

Then their hair grew out like jigsaw pieces as the decade
kinked and snaked . . . until it was Saturday night
in small-town downtown, all of them piled
like marsupials in the backseat's pouch. Their car
would be hawing at the curbside while the eldest
bopped into the liquor store for some Wild Irish Rose,
his strides filigreed with a little hiccup
every time he shucked the ballast of his Dingo boot.
Later, when they passed out where the rumpus rooms

gave way between the speakers, or when their car
barreled into the lone tree that stood its ground,
I saw how power suffered its ignominies
without blustering or braking—think of Cesare Borgia
leading the cathedral's *Christ Have Mercy*
in a tin mask after syphilis wrecked his face.
These were the ghosts of men who stood at the altar
wearing spurs and daggers underneath their pleats,
Romans come back now all leather fringe and eyelids

.   .   .

drooping in a rogue half-sleep. The miracle
was how by Sunday mass their mother always
righted them again. And bullied their hair
into nests like squirrels made, and strapped their neckties
tight to hold up their heads. Then came the rumbling
that was their singing, before the uncle's name
drew through us like a knife, the uncle whose red cap
meant willingness to shed blood for the faith,
though at the time all I knew was its astonishing color.

Nathan's

When church was done, what my mother wanted
was a cup of coffee not made from dust.
And my father woke hungry from his dreams
of waffle-cut fries in their cardboard boat
and blintzes and bagels and burgundy meats
distinguished by their mottlings of fat.

By day, its neon resembled barbed wire:
this mutant hybrid of hot dog and man.
Inside, the hairnet battalions rafted
potato knishes through white-water grease
and tonged the wieners into buns' white seams,
where each sprawled like a lurid odalisque.

And when I'd spent too long with the gray gum
daubing the table's baroque underside,
my father would dredge his pockets for change
he presented in his palm, so that I'd
go away, leaving him and my mother
to bite down on their coffee cups in peace.

And that's how I left them, for the arcade
at Nathan's Famous, for gunning down ducks
and steering the roadster over the grains
of film loops reckless with their apple carts
and mules. Soon it would be risky trying
to go back for extra dimes—my mother

. . .

would test my head-sweat with her hand, pronounce
that I'd had enough. So I paced myself,
rationing coins, saving my last to rouse
the Gypsy in her dusty velvet booth.
Drowsily, her clay claw nudged the tarot
until a chit fluttered into this world

like a leaf. Predicting love or travel,
though *Time to go* is what it meant—who knows
how she knew when my father's cigarette
was closing on his knuckles? My parents
gazing, rapt, at nothing, maybe even
holding hands—and this is what appalled me,

this idea that someday I too might think
one decent cup of coffee was enough.
Sometimes I steered for the mule on purpose,
just to see if it had guts, but the hide
always turned into a whirling gray blotch
without answering me: *Enough what? What?*

II

They say that God is everywhere and yet we always think of Him as somewhat of a recluse.

—EMILY DICKINSON

White Bird/Black Drop

1

The snowy egret's not extinct
no matter how archaic it may seem:
its crest a rack of spiky feathers
that would ornament a woman's hat
in another era. A less functional era.
Where the hat would go with a backless gown
showing off the woman's spine,
her legs hidden under fabric folds
made sumptuous by light.
And we imagine her legs have grace
when in fact they could be sticks,
like the stick legs of the snowy egret,
which are covered in black chitin
that erupts into bright yellow feet.
Lavishness where it makes no sense,
buried in the mud. So Audubon
painted the bird on shore, giving
the legs the illusion of movement—
& I don't understand: how the feet can lift
when the legs appear to have no meat in them
at all. Their carcasses
littered the park where I worked,
where the birds flew into power lines
that sliced across the marshes.
And the legs took only a day in the sun
before becoming dry enough
to be set out in the Nature Center,
in a box where children stuck their hands

before they looked—a game
about what we imagine from forms that go unseen.
But before too long the legs were banished,
after a woman complained that her son
had been tricked into touching a dead thing
& could not be consoled for weeks.

2

Now the era wants us working
in order to improve ourselves:
forget Coleridge wandering the upland
stoned out of his head, forget him
& his years in the spare bedroom
at the surgeon Gillman's house
where Gillman doled the Black Drop out
to every day's white page.
The Black Drop, cottage industry of widows:
opium dissolved in quince fruit juice,
& is it wrong to lament its passing
along with extinct words like *quince fruit juice*?
But the snowy egret's not extinct, no matter
how dead it sounds like it should be.
And for that you can thank the functional era
for having no patience with ornament:
so women give up fancy hats
& the birds return to the wayside marsh,
where they dot the green like clods of foam
bobbing amongst the empty bottles.
Once when she was really flying
my girlfriend bought a velvet hat,
a black pillbox with one white plume
shooting straight up from the forehead.
This she wore with rubber boots
to bang my door at ten P.M.,
my friend plotched on cough syrup,
her mind wandering the upland.

And now that she's dried out,
she fears for her liver; sometimes
(pressing the phone to it) she'll ask,
long distance, what I think (she thinks
the hat got left on a Greyhound bus).
I think, *Yeah, but remember the fun*
we had walking the stiff plumes of our hair
through fresh snow glowing lilac in the moonlight?
But she says no; those nights were tragic
and she can't remember anything.

3

Those years my friend gave to Robitussin
I spent chasing after men on bikes,
the loud machines they wore as ornaments
between their legs. They all had the long
black-clad legs of the egret—
spread, slightly bent, from the low-slung seat.
And I would have liked to have been one myself
but part of me wanted to stay in the bed,
my spine a white curl replicating
the S-curves of the canyon road,
my plumage perhaps a camisole
with one torn strap. But the choice was either
him or her, looker or looked-at,
subject or object, you could not be both.
And me being pigeon-toed & flighty, unable
to hold anything upright with my bad legs . . .
well, it figures I'd come to land here
where the cedars drip into Ellis Cove
& the long-legged birds stand stock-still
on the stumps; that's how they disguise themselves.
As I'm likewise disguised in a porkpie hat,
binoculars my only ornament besides the clear drop
clinging to the bulb of my nose-tip.
Above the cove, the shoreline road
hugs the curl of the embankment.
And the guys (who would be geezers now)
rumble along it on their Honda Goldwings.

4

Audubon's most famous painting
I must have looked at a hundred times
before I noticed the tiny hunter
approaching from across the marsh.
Meanwhile the bird keeps the black drop of its eye
steady on us, terrifyingly steady,
as if he accepts this one long moment—
Perfect Beauty—for whatever comes next.
And isn't that why the guys all lit out
on their bikes: to stop time
while they were still in their best feathers?
Shaggy at the head and neck,
they let the whole world enter them—
the speed, the green, the trash-strewn marsh—
looker & looked-at blurred into one thing.
One time when I asked the bad-boy poet
to read his poem about the egret, which I love,
it was not his refusal that angered me
so much as the way that he'd aged
so much better than me. And now that he's dead
sometimes I'll spot a beauty like his
riding crosstown on the stuttering bus.
Like Coleridge on the deck of the *Speedwell*,
sailing toward Malta in his sealskin coat,
though in this case of course it's a black leather jacket,
one of those portable black caves of sleep.
Look at him dozing, hunched into his collar.
Look at him hunched into his wrecked good looks.

If he looks out the window, I bet what he'll notice
is the sky's bearing down now, as if it might snow.
The crushed cans singing in the ditches
& the trash bags pinned to the cyclone fence.
But he won't see the bird
in its grand bright whiteness—
hunkered like foam-clod, luffing in the wind.

5

Getting back, at last, to the salt marsh where I worked:
in the California summers, botulism
rampaged through the ponds.
It made the birds' necks fold
& their long legs double up
as they dragged their shaggy haunches
through the shoreline's stinking dust.
The snowy egret I found
was long past hope——whenever
I found a sick bird on the trail
I was supposed to take it back to the office
where one of the men would break its neck
to keep the disease from spreading.
All right, then. That's what I'd do.
I carried the egret clamped under my arm,
because I'd read that given a chance
it might spear me in the eye
with its black beak. Strange
how it knew the eyeball was soft
& crucial to its being seen, & knew
how the viewer produces the viewed
in a miracle of transference.
Black drop inside of yellow drop,
black drop inside of bluish-gray:
we studied each other while the trapped head twitched.
And by the time I got back
all the men had gone home, so I killed the bird
the way they did, by taking its head

in the cave of my hand & making my thumb
& forefinger a collar around its neck.
Then I spun the body until it went limp—
this was easier than I expected.
The late sun was broadcasting
gold light on the marsh, & I did not think of Coleridge
& what the dead bird meant to him.
Instead, in that moment, I felt like a man,
or how I imagined a man might feel.
A delusion, of course, & soon the sun closed shop,
& then all I felt was sadness
for what the world had made of me.

After Larry Levis

On the High Suicide Rate of Dentists

It's no surprise, when you think about what the teeth
are the ramparts of: slippery slope
leading to the gullet. Little jagged-edged ivory
makers of sameness, the Bolsheviks of the dining room:

take the lobster tail or the prime rib,
put in your mouth and chew them awhile
and all class distinctions—whether deep-fried or drowning in
    butter—
quickly become moot. But any actual tears

are hard drops to explain, especially coming from someone
like the one who played "novelty music"
when he chopped the fillings out of me.
Guitarzan. How lighthearted he seemed

as he chimed along with Jane's falsetto yodeling.
And though you might think gastroenterologists
would wear the crown of their despairs,
at least they witness how bygones can be bygones

and how the burden can be released. Versus this
perpetual going-in, which is always the scariest part
of the story: *Give up hope all ye who enter here.*
Even the radishes are doomed, cut so painstakingly into roses.

So maybe part of their sadness comes from the sushi
assembled to look like the stained glass at Chartres.
Or the crown roast whose bones wear those paperboy caps
while ever so eager the knife goes in.

Little Phallus Song (for John Berryman)

> . . . the great red joy a pecker ought to be
> to pump a woman ragged . . .
> —JOHN BERRYMAN

Not having one on my own personage
I think of the dolls that commandeered my youth
and how I pushed their ornate carriage
up and down the cracked sidewalk, my hands both
on the handle. Call me torturer,
terrorist, rotator of limbs till they popped
from the sockets—even armless and hole-hipped,
they knew that I was their good mother.
What toes remained I gnawed until their feet were stubbed
and their heads I rubbed, and rubbed, and rubbed
until the hair—signified by an orange or brown paint—
abraded to bald under all my petting,
all my fawning, all my *Darling*,
lamb chop, don't you look feverish, don't you look faint.

Nudism in America

Lying in the hammock strung between
the dead apple tree and the half-dead plum,
I'm reading the selected letters of Keats
in a used paperback that I bought for a dollar.
Another dollar bought this postcard
that I'm using for a bookmark:
four naked people on a deck backdropped
by an expanse of piney woods. A black-
and-white photo from the A-bomb era,
colorized in radioactive tones,
so the two men look like orange ex-Nazis,
and the women, fugitives of a different sort,
from a beach-blanket movie: cat's-eye sunglasses,
kerchiefs, lipstick, hair done up in flips.
And every few pages I find myself flipping
back to wherever they last held my place:
Whenever I am among women, says Keats,
I have evil thoughts and malice spleen.
He vows never to spend time with ladies
unless they are handsome, uh-oh, nudist red alert:
your women are lumpy and their small breasts droop.
So isn't it good, to see also the gusto
with which the men show off for their amusement:
one does a handstand, the other a squat thrust
while the women toss their heads and laugh.
Keats's America was a gray mass in the distance,
a menacing cloud colorized in fake hues;
I cannot put faith in any report from the settlements—
this he wrote to his brother George,
who'd emigrated to Pennsylvania's piney woods.

Where George lost his shirt in a riverboat scheme,
hoodwinked by that gray mass, John James Audubon,
before the latter struck it rich by painting birds
in poses that've always struck me as some avian variant
of soft-core porn. Something about the birds' necks being bent
backward, to expose the underside of their throats,
making them look too eager to be ravished,
too sexually alert. But I can read sex
into even the limbs of the trees,
which is why I suspect that some trick card
must be up the nudists' absent sleeves.
Because arousal is something
we expect the body to betray
and the fact that theirs do not is, let's face it,
weird (we're not talking one woman alone
with a bowl of fruit). Yet I can rest
their crotch-fur against a poem's
made sweet moan copied out in a letter,
and I can take the scrotums just edging out
from beyond the horizon of nudist skin
and I can fold them into *Bright star!*
would I were steadfast as thou art—
after all, isn't this America, this pot where everything
is supposed to melt? And when I've had enough
nineteenth-century diction for one hammock sitting,
I'll let the years be pressed flat like a leaf.
Old World and New, the word and the flesh,
birds and boobs and all of us sleeping
here in my backyard, the nudists inserted
here, between two of John Keats's many thighs.

Life in the Year 2000

I flew a spaceship past the tallest skyscraper
and smokestacks unfurling a curlicue soot—
a future that came when the school substitute
ran out of ideas except crayons and paper:

Draw a picture of life in the year 2000.
Then "42" flashed up on my brain's marquee,
because forty-two was how old I'd be,
nearly as old as my grandmother was, bunioned

and cabbage-scented. But once she had sailed on a ship
of her own, and the strange word *steerage*
drew me its own picture. Of her as the one with her grip
on the wheel, her breasts in a stiff beige

Old World underthing while the boat came
onward, toward the city. In the year 2000 we would wear
spacesuits made from some scientific new polymer
like latex, which already had a garment to proclaim:

The Living Bra. My own breasts were not yet on the radar,
not yet did their presence require a word,
yet this *living* made me think they'd move of their own accord
like gyroscopes steering the flight of the ship. The future

would be stranger than steerage: the farther we'd travel
the more ridiculous we'd look. And just to be safe,
when commanded, I always drew in myself
in the driver's side window, profiled in its hole.

.　.　.

Then I had no breasts and no legs to worry about.
And even my head was covered in a shiny silver helmet.

Poem Without Breasts

The world has countless board feet of lumber,
crustaceans, skyscrapers, sword ferns
and sabers—what I'm driving at

is anything that does not suggest a bulbous shape.
Because I have used the word far too often—
or so says my critic, who once had a sty

go away when he swabbed it with mother's milk.
Go away: to wherever it is that sties come from,
though in this case the milk did not come from me,

me never spritzing like vaudeville seltzer
or a baroque fountain in a quaint Italian city.
My mother favored cylinders with plastic bags inside

so air wouldn't enter the baby and cause it to explode:
I remember how on TV a scientist stood, pointering
gingerly, at a diagram of the perilously bloated child.

Yet there is much in this world that does not
feed on milk: the overpass, the Douglas fir,
the steel I-beam, though its birth can be traced

backward, to the foundry's blazing bowl.
Origins are globes, and though the statue of the Virgin
may have started as a block of stone

. . .

her shining moment comes when she starts expressing
her liquid of choice: either blood or tears or milk
in drops whose surface curves the rigid world.

Sure the gland can be bound, as Billy Tipton bound hers
when she took up the trumpet and life as a man.
And not until it came time to cremate him

did anyone think to open up the shirt. Which made
all the straight stuff crack like his wife's voice
when the unspoken finally assumed its rightful place.

Given Unlimited Space, the Dead Expand Limitlessly

What do the daylilies say in December?
Their only tongue is the language of stalks.
Rained on and battered. Their color no color.
But what's hard on the eye is good for what hulks
underground—in their case, not even a bulb.
Just the rhizome that harbors the brain of the flower.
Whose remnants are bony, aslant in the mulch,
crisscrossed, Euclidian. But they will not bow
the whole way down; they will not worship, they will not rot.
Instead, they tilt like mannequins without their wigs
intertwined in the window of a bankrupt shop
whose dust is sliced by ancient legs.
And even when new leaves shoot from the thawing earth—
they'll preside here nude, not giving up their turf.

Fresh Water and Salt

When we were young girls and swam naked in Turkey Lake
we were like animals: our legs were thickly furred.
We took the trees' rustling for a sign of their watching.
Even the limestone drooled from its mouth cracks.

But then I got real: it was only lake ledges, dripping—
rainwater, sweat of moss, and dew.
Maybe a man hid behind a birch's pale skin
and I saw him, once. The rest, my ego running wild.

Still, it's the roundabout way that I'm taking to the island
that is Indian land, where I lay down without my shirt.
This is years from the lake, and the water is salt
when a rockslide clatters off the bluff.

Make the clatter a sign of the watchers come forward—
in the calm that comes after, I can hear their feet.
But the trees have long since surrendered their trench coats
and gone back to being simple trees.

First thought, *I've grown old;* second thought is the cops
but I keep my eyes closed to stall their skirmish
over me. Time clicks like their footsteps as they come close—
until a musty breath whelms down my face.

Now hold it there, freeze-frame, while I look up
at the sun's corona on a mule deer's chin.
Chewing some fox grass, regarding me only
because on this wild shore I am strange.

In the Confessional Mode, with a Borrowed Movie Trope

. . . and then there is the idea of another life
of which this outward life is only an expression,
the way the bag floating round in the alley
traces out the shape of wind
but is not wind. In a fleabag hotel
in Worcester, Mass., a man is dying,
muscles stiff, their ropes pulled taut,
his voice somewhere between a honk and whisper.
But float down through the years, many years,
and it's us, meaning me and the man
as a boy who's upstairs in the house
where I've finagled my deflowering.
Maybe finagled. Hard to say if it's working.
It reminds me of trying to cram a washrag
down a bottleneck—you twist and twist
to make it reach, but it does not,
and in the end the inside of me
was not wiped clean. Oh I was once
in such a hurry. The job had to be done
before the pot roast was, his stepmother
thumping the ceiling under us: *Whatever
you're doing, you better get out
of your sister's room.* But her voice
carried more of the wasp's irritation
than the hornet's true rage, so we forged on—
while our jury of trusty busty Barbies
perched on their toes, their gowns iridescent,
a sword of gray light coming through the curtain crack
and knighting me where I contorted

on the rug. And it's clear to me still,
what I wanted back then; namely, my old life
cut up into shreds so I could get on
with my next. But the boy was only
halfway hard, no knife edge there,
though the rest of him looked like it were bronze,
with muscles rumpling his dark-gold skin.
Meaning this is a story about beauty after all.
And when the roast was ready, I slipped outside,
where November dusk was already sifting down
into the ballrooms underneath the trees.
It was time to go home to my own dinner,
the ziti, the meatballs, *Star Trek* on TV,
but how could I sit there, familiar among them,
now that I was this completely different thing?
Sweat was my coat as I flew from his house
while the brakes of my ten-speed sang like geese.
But now it's his voice that resembles a honk
in a room where the empty amber vials
rattle underneath his narrow bed. Meaning
he's trying hard to take himself out.
And while I have as yet no theory
to unlock the secret forces of the earth, still
I think there's a reason why the boy and I,
when we grew up, both got stuck
with the same disease. Meaning the stiffness,
the spasms, the concrete legs—
oh I was once in such a hurry. Now
my thighs are purple from all the drugs
I'm shooting in, & I don't even want to know
how the boy looks wracked and wrecked.
Sometimes in the midst of making love
that kind of body will come floating in,

but quickly I'll nudge it away in favor of
the airbrushed visions. But not him,
the young him, the brass plate of whose belly
would be more lovely than I could bear,
though in chaster moments I will visit
that alcove of me where his torso is struck
by all the dark-gold light that still slants in.
Oh we are blown, we are bags,
we are moved by such elegant chaos.
Call it god. Only because it is an expletive that fits.
His body, his beauty, all fucked up now.
God. Then the air cuts out, and then we drop.

Fubar

For Paul Guest

For starters, scratch the woman weeping over her dead cat—
sorry, but pet death barely puts the needle in the red zone.
And forget about getting brownie points
for any heartbreak mediated by the jukebox.
See the leaves falling; isn't this the trees' way of telling us to just
    buck up?

Oh they are right: their damage is so much greater than our
    damage.
I mean, none of my body parts have actually dropped off.
And when the moon is fat and handsome, I know we should be
    grateful
that its face is only metaphor; it has no teeth to chew us out.
In fact, the meadow isn't spattered with the tatters of our guts.

But in last night's hypnagogic dreamscape where I went
to collect some data. Where I was just getting into the swing of
    things
tranquillity-wise. Then this kid came rolling through the moonlight
in a bed with lots of Rube Goldberg traction rigging.
And it was a kid like you, some kid with a broken neck.

And maybe beauty is medicine quivering on the spoon
but surely you have noticed—the goat painted on the famous old
    Greek urn
is headed to the slaughter. And don't get me started
on the wildflowers or they will lead me to the killer bees.
And that big ol' moon will lead to a cross-section of the spinal cord.

. . .

And the trees to their leaves, all smushed in the gutter.
And the gutter to the cat squashed flat as a hotcake.
And the hotcake to the grits, and the grits to the South,
where the meadows were once battlefields.
Where a full moon only meant a better chance of being shot.

But come on, the sun is rising, I'll put a bandage on my head,
and we'll be like those guys at the end of the movie—
you take this crutch made from a stick.
For you the South is a mess, what with its cinders and its
    smoldering.
And looky, looky here at me: I'm playing the piccolo.

For the Pileated Woodpecker and Its Cousin, the Ivory-billed, Who May or May Not Be Extinct

So ta-*dah:* Here's the moment to which we've been brung—
but right off the bat, don't things get snarled.
The moment feels right, but I'm not sure about *brung,*
a folksy idiom to brush against the modern, which is our way,
the modern way, you know:
the old barn parked beside the SUV.
Or the pitchfork the parent stabs through the Gameboy.
The salt pork completely savaged by the microwave.

That's what's wrong with the moment; it is always so shiny
when it pulls up like a white limo at the curb.
Or to use a supporting argument,
from inside the car by the Skokomish River
where Jim says, "What would you call that giant woodpecker?"
and I say, "What giant woodpecker?" but *poof*—
the bird has flown before I can fix it
(the vision of it, the real of it) with any sort of toxic nimbus

from my brain's aerosol can with the ball inside it, ticking.
Other times I've heard its knocking,
the loud hard gavel of *momentmoment,*
but in the woods I tracked down just a feathery blur, a black wig
    flying.
And was it only a moment ago I was dressed so chic
and now I'm taking those same clothes to the thrift store
in plastic bags, like a body being dumped?
One night I even performed the experiment

.   .   .

of looking into the mirror and saying the word *now,*
only the now that was said was the now that was gone
and did I feel it? could I feel it?
Here's what happens: the tongue knocks on the palate
before lying down in the jaw's own swamp,
then the *ow*-sound flies from the nest box of the throat,
and the self ends up a doofus, standing there
breathing with an open mouth.

Bulletin from Somewhere up the Creek

Luckily, it's shallow enough that I can pole my rubber boat—
don't ask what happened to the paddle. Anywhere is lovely
if you look hard enough: the scum on the surface
becomes a lace of tiny flowers.
In the space between cedars, a half-moon slides
across a sky colored like the inside of a clam.
Two terns slice it with their sharp beaks,
gape-mouthed and wheeling and screaming like cats.

See, nature is angry, I said to myself: *Nature
is just an ice pick with wings.* Then a weasel or something
poked its head through the muck, looked around for a while
before submerging again. And not even bumping
the ketchup squeeze bottle seemed to disturb it,
nor was it afraid to lose itself in this brown soup.
Or maybe this was just a very large rat—still,
why should its example be of any less worth?

Ah, my friends, I could tell you my troubles
but is that why you came? Sure, it stinks here—
the best birding is done in foul-smelling places.
So far I've seen the hawk circling, the kingfisher chuckling
before smashing itself breast-first in the muck.
I've watched the blue heron standing on just one leg
until it found something half rotten to spear. Then swallowing
with a toss of its head, as if this were a meal for kings.

Second Poem Without Breasts

In my first poem without breasts, what I forgot
is this: how they could kill you. It isn't a joke
or maybe it is—the cartoon coyote
blown up by the cannonball. The Playmate of the Month
is a time bomb ticking, and shouldn't someone
tell the boy with his flashlight, under the covers?
When he fixes his gerund to the unfortunate noun
(flogging the bishop, boxing the clown)
for a piffle of time he wants to be a dead man
(so *poof!* you're a dead man). But then the kid
wants to come back; how come *he* gets to come back
when Playmate, honey, you're like the *Hindenburg*
when all the molecules inside the blimp went crazy?
So the doctor says, Infiltrating ductal carcinoma
and *poof*—there is no coming back. Was that
what you yearned for, back when you willed them,
one summer-camp summer, to appear upon your ribs?
Now you'd auction them off to the highest bidder:
let them be wineskins, or a bagpipe or two;
if there was a bone in the house you could sharpen enough
you'd even do the job yourself. Goodbye
to fertility goddesses with their high buttocks—
from here on out, you're eating chalk and dust.
Even a feather-stuffed pillow will be too much fluff;
like a yogi, you'll lay your head on top a rock.
A jagged one, so the dream digs its knuckle in your skull.
Or a smooth one, for the solace of its hard gray face.
Or if that kind of Zen doesn't suit you, Bunny,
you can praise the knives as they go about their work.

Making the scar that'll run like the ridge
where the coyote stops with her nose lifted
as the fuse burns through, as she listens to the tick.

News from the Republic of Housecoats

They are almost extinct now, like the snail darter:
those shiny, knee-length, synthetic pup tents
whose texture was that of a quilted fish—
though the dry fish fades
while their loud colors persisted
through the long years of several wars.

In my childhood those houses were scary to enter:
a woman ensconced with a net on her head
to cover the curlers while a soap opera played
and the mother smoked, or did not,
as was her preference.
But usually she did, if only to change

the quality of light filtering in through the blinds.
A pack of some now-extinct brand on the TV tray:
fiberglass impregnated with a mountain scene.
Chesterfield. The Caucasus. And the actors
moved on the TV as if underwater
while the plot, in its riverbed, ran on and on.

But all that is dying, as the rivers are dying,
as the vegetation is dying beside the old smelters
in old newsreels from cities
with a gray rind of snow
where nothing is as shiny as an underwater fish—
though the light may be as filmy and the women as wavering.

. . .

Outside, they wear socks with their weird short boots.
And kerchiefs that hide all the news
in their brows. Their wool coats
are horsehair. The dictator, dead.
See them boarding a bus that's shaped like a bread loaf,
leaving us here, in our sweatpants, now.

On the Rhythmic Nature of Obscure Toil

So you write one poem, then another,
until your stack is big enough to bind with a black
spring clip. If you were Emily Dickinson
(but there is no chance that you're Emily Dickinson)
you'd have poked a sharp needle through the sheaf.
Then laid it to rest in an underwear drawer
until you died of glomerulonephritis:
a disease, alas, with too many syllables
to suit your common meter. And when sister Vinnie
discovers your cache, what do you care?
You just wish you'd sat for another daguerreotype
besides that one with your hair so severely parted,
signifying the pre–central plumbing era
and its omnipresent oily scalp.
Then hair mousse comes along
and the thread through the sheaf becomes this spring clip
made by a woman imprisoned in China.
One minute she's doing Tai Chi in the park,
making Fair Lady wrists when a cop steps up,
calls her pose dissident, and slaps on the cuffs.
Then for all minutes after, she's sticking these wires
into the black triangular piece,
so many per hour her fingers are flayed
like brushes dipped in rust-red paint.
And you, you thought you were just writing a poem
without the crutch of Emily Dickinson's beat,
her thump-thump-thump-thump/thump-thump-thump
that can be sung to "Swing Low Sweet Chariot"
or "When the Saints Go Marching In."
But since you didn't want that to help you along,

you were just fidgeting, scratching your head,
absentmindedly staring out of the window,
and while you were gone, look:
someone left these bloody prints across the page.

III

And to die is different from what any one supposed,
and luckier.
—WALT WHITMAN

The man who has fed the chicken every day throughout its life at
last wrings its neck instead, showing that more refined views as to
the uniformity of nature would have been useful to the chicken.
—BERTRAND RUSSELL

Urban Legend

Like many stories, this one begins with Jesus—
well, he sure looks like Jesus, this guy pulled over by the ditch.
Let's say the tarp has blown off the back of his Isuzu pickup.
Let's say that the apostles are slowly rising heavenward.

See them twisting in the thermals, in this sky that's not a joke
even if these fugitives could figure in a gag's protracted setup.
Calling for the hauling of twelve helium-filled desire dolls—
to a toga party. See how the apostles all have boners underneath
     their robes.

And isn't that like me, to put the *boners* into play,
however inappropriate, when this is not a joke.
This is not a joke because the story wants to go into the record.
Yes, it does want. The story has a little mind that thinks.

And the mind sends its ambassadors: these poodles nuked in
     microwaves,
bonsai kittens, sewer crocodiles, rats suckled in maternity wards.
I believe in the fatal hairdo just for the love of saying *fatal hairdo.*
And I believe in the stolen kidney because I too have woken up
     with something missing.

But I haven't spoken yet of the rapture, another word whose
     saying
is like dancing at a toga party after downing many shots.
Because who hasn't tried to pull their arms from the sleeves of
     gravity's lead coat?
Who doesn't have at least one pair of wax wings out in the garage?

. . .

So back to Jesus, back to daylight, and you can make the dimwit
    me
who launches herself into the updraft of the rapture
and goes sailing straight through the story's sunroof. Above, the
    bonsai kittens
pad the sky as cherubim. Below me, hairdos right and left are going
    up in smoke.

Now the apostles are storming heaven, the Isuzu's motor's ticking,
while the left hand of Jesus forms a ledge above his brow.
And you, earth angel, fear not my crash landing in the diamond
    lane—
the vinyl men are full of noble gas, and I'm rising on my balsa
    wings.

By Edvard Munch, Two Paintings
Thirty Years Apart on the Same Jetty

Everything has loosened, both the sunset and the sea,
your hair wound backward into the follicles.
Gone, your body's involutions;
your hands are pale tubes like soiled white socks
as if you were pupating and the moth inside you
were about to be unleashed. Already
you've pressed what your hands now are
against what used to be your ears
as if you expected a crack when your body unhusks;
in fact you *want* a loud crack, if you gotta be a moth
be a terrible moth, go on and curdle the sky
and make it rain down molten spit.

But look at what happens, how the sky cools down,
how the sea grows calm enough to reflect a simple house
even if it can't handle the risen moon just yet.
And look what those two strangers turned into,
they who once stepped from the vanishing point
in long black coats. They were only girls after all,
who now stand beside you—
turns out neither of them held a scythe.

Sorry: no scythe, no molten spit,
no wiggly black tunic in life-size inflatable format
sold at the mall at Spencer Gifts.
And you are bitter about the moth business
being a bum steer, in a blink you'd trade
blue-ribbon mental health for even a T-shirt version

of immortality; you'd gladly swap
all your windblown blond hair, which at least isn't braided
in pigtails like these other two, and by God you're glad for that.

A Simple Camp Song

In the days of yore, three handsome drunks
took me to sea until my jigging hook was swallowed.
I reeled its line around a plywood chock
until the big fish hovered at the ceiling of the water.

I know this sounds like a fable, so let it be a fable
in the rain where we hunched underneath our stupid hats.
We didn't have a gun, so one of the drunks leaned out
and drove a gaffing hook under its jawbone.

A loud *whump* from the transom when the rope played out;
then the little boat stood on its hind end. We rose up
with the bench seats pinned behind our knees
and hung in the air until the boat sat down again.

And nobody's lungs were inundated by the sea
in this soft-core, cloud-upholstered version of the past.
Someone merely pulled the starter and we towed the fish to shore,
where it sprawled on the wet sand, bigger than a woman.

I know a fable would have coughed up a pearl or a word
but the fish was a fish, lying there, not speaking.
Its lips did move in a mockery of speech,
its gills a set of louvers, opening and closing.

Then the drunks found sticks and I did too
and we brought them down on the shovel of its skull.
But the fish wouldn't die until I put some weight behind the stick,
until I jumped with my upswing, like a primitive.

. . .

Buh went the stick. It felt all right to be barbaric,
to be cut from the same cloth as the wilderness itself.
But soon a birding group appeared on the bluff
and stripped all the teeth off the gears inside their lungs.

The drunks were coming sober and the screaming made them look
down at their hands, streaked with red fish blood.
The birders wanted us to find a quicker way to kill the fish—
Okay, you try, we said.

Then it drops like a curtain, the heavy velvet of dys-memory.
I guess the sandpipers wobbled in the tide pools in the rocks.
The birders withered back into the spaces in the brush.
And someone cut off the halibut's cheeks.

The reason why it's vague is: all I wanted was the drunks,
bunch of snaggle-toothed losers who lived in trailers in the woods.
In those days I was drawn to the wind-chapped hand.
Good Lord, how they stunk.

Question: how big does a stick have to be to be a club?
Answer: at least as big around as a small man's wrist.
Too big, and the club starts to turn into a log.
And the drunks start to stagger when they it raise for their blows.

So how far back for yore? First the story needs to skip
the part where the club has bits of brain stuck to the wood.
Instead, cut to the evening when we chopped the fish in pieces
and ate them fried in butter that left a halo around our mouths.

Valentine Delivered by a Horde of Birds, Some Years After Its Original Inception

This time of year, the birds descend,
re-leafing the trees with their dark forms.
They preside from their branches,
a quorum of judges—
starlings and blackbirds and grackles, I guess,
though there's not enough wattage today in the sky
to light their blue heads. All the circuits
are already being used to amplify their chatter.

And you will remember how we once saw them streaming
over the lake where the poison particles
lie buried in the silt. How we pulled off the road
to watch them land by the hundreds
in the nude oaks lining the dead cornfield,
you will remember. How we forsook the car
to stand underneath, the sound
like every fence gate on the planet, swinging.

I was going to call it love, but it is not love, or is it:
this place where instinct takes us
under inappropriate conditions.
But in the end there were only so many places on you
where I was willing to put my mouth—
so we got back in the car and just sat there, listening.
Which, admit it,
was more erotic than the kissing.

.　　.　　.

And so it was with the birds today,
though you were not here and I was only under them
to drag the trash can to the curb. Sure, I know
what those drops were that fell on me, but still:
the sound, and even the wetness,
drove my heart wild. Oh love I know
it would not be so thrilling if it didn't also terrify, this loud mess
we cannot keep ourselves from entering.

Book of Bob

1. Invocation with language imprecise

Now he's dead, and so I guess
I could have him say anything I want.
My father's mouth I could fill with flowers
but beauty meant less to him than plain old bread.
So let it be bread then, let him be Bob,
let everything go by its plainest name—
including the dirt and the bones inside it,
the secret bones inside the dirt.
Many jockeys have come to unseemly ends,
many horses were sent down to their graves
when their intricate unlucky knuckles unknitted
down a muddy track's backstretch.
But some of them rose and hobbled on,
their manes awash with blood and sweat,
the lather running from their mouths,
the ridden, the risen, the riven, the roans—
which he called *ponies*
though they weren't all that small.

2. Brief political chronology with Judith Campbell Exner

As a young man, he'd been a communist,
back in the days of the shadow of Eugene Debs.
He was a Democrat until John Kennedy's mistress
testified on TV, her dark glasses glistening like scarabs.
So Camelot had mob connections.
My father sobbed at the mention of Sam Giancana's name.
Time zipped, and the Soviets turned back into Russians,
and Betty Grable turned into some dame
in a big hat, jetting off to negotiate.
But by then he was old, holed up in his bed,
jockeying channels as the night grew late
and tongue-lashing the TV set.
The new White House press secretary he
dismissed, saying: *What the hell kind of name is Dee Dee?*

3. Epiphany with a blood-sugar spike

Only when he thought he was dying, did he turn religious:
Never believed in God, but maybe I've been oblivious.

Turned out the raptures came from his fouled-up blood
and, once they dialyzed him, he quit pestering God.

Then three times a week everyone made him schlep
back over that river, on whose far shore a man could sleep

without even taking off his shoes.
Who cares if you came back with all of your toes

to the Naugahyde harbor of the La-Z-Boy
from which he called to ask what I did all day?

White noise for his kidney, I said I was typing
like a court clerk or Girl Friday, something

on which I thought he could get a grip.
And then he said: *Ah, now I get it—*

in high school you were good at that.

4. At the Dowdle Funeral Home

Centuries ago, we'd have washed him with vinegar,
but now we women sigh and fidget.
Sister coos like an injured bird
while I press his cheek
to see if he's been painted.
Secret work, the face filled with wax,
I wanted to feel
this monster business of the body.
Go on, he telepaths, knowing I am that kind of child.
But is overruled by molecules building their scaffolds
out of static. We are soldiers
unused to such strict standing,
eyes boring ahead like invisible tusks
before the task is given. If there were dust
on the sills we could have addressed it,
but we had no rags or lemon juice.
And without something to wash, we women
were lost. Without a wound to dress,
a floor to sweep, a child to nurse, an onion to chop—
the kind of work we'd come prepared for.

5. Canticle from the Book of Bob

We hired the men to carry the coffin,
we hired a woman to sing in our stead.
We hired a limo, we hired a driver,
we hired each lily to stand with its head

held up and held open while scripture was read.
We hired a dustpan, we hired a broom
to sweep up the pollen that fell in the room
where we'd hired some air

to draw out the stale chord
from the organ we hired.
And we hired some tears because our own eyes were tired.

The pulpit we hired, we hired the priest
to say a few words about the deceased,

and money changed hands
and the process was brief.
We said, "Body of Christ."
Then we hired our grief.

We hired some young men to carry the coffin,
we hired a woman to sing for his soul—
we hired the limo, we hired the driver,
then we hired the ground and we hired the hole.

6. Outtake in which no words are said

Trouble was, his passions did not last too long
like the year he tilled the lawn and grew tall corn

that the raccoons broke his heart by eating.
What spring expected, fall defeated.

Once when we were kids he bought us rods and reels
and took us fishing in the Hudson. But all we caught was eels

and were too horrified to take the hook out of the mouth.
In the end, he cut the line and left them on the wharf.

7. Epilogue with a deep image

But how can this be—my father did not walk—
his feet wobbled uncertainly beneath his ankles.
Yet here he is, gesturing with his cigar's wet stalk
over our heads, at the arched limbs of the maples
whose trunks line the road that climbs toward our house,
their foliage the same bright color as his shoes.
A pair of cherry-tone loafers in which he scuffs,
though sometimes a couple wild steps will break loose
as if music had struck him as we walk along.
He's telling me how he'd been sad when I was young—
happy pills: that's what came of the doctor visit.
And as for the end of the story, he flaps his hand: *eff.*
One day I flushed them down the toilet.
I decided my life was happy enough.

My Eulogy Was Deemed Too Strange

My father battled two fire-breathing white owls
that night with his sword, though he was small
and they taller than the turrets—his blade
swung only as far as their thighs.
He was dressed like an Apollo astronaut
and we were driving toward the pancake house

when we saw the castle, beset by flames.
That's when my father pulled off the road
and got embroiled in what this is: first dream
I ever dreamed. Come morning, I wanted to ask
if the fire had happened, if the others had seen
his silver boots, as delicate as carpet slippers.

But I kept my mouth shut, because—though I couldn't
distinguish the owls from the rest of the weirdness
that passes for life at the age of five—I knew
how it sounded to sound like a fool. And now
I know this: that the castle stood in the same spot
by the rise in the road to the pancake house

as where we laid him out when his time came.
Not a castle at all but a funeral home
in whose next room resided a dead fireman
whose brethren arrived in dress uniform
and paid their respects to my dad's coffin
until they realized their mistake. Outside,

.　　.　　.

the fire truck's lights swept across the wet window,
making our faces glow and dim and glow again.
But my mother looked nervous when I tried to explain
how it started in flames in the place where it ended.
As if she could see me chest-deep in the pulpit
with the book of Nostradamus and a tarot deck.

So at mass the next day I held my tongue
and used it only as a platform for the wafer, the body of Christ,
about whom my father had his doubts. I just wish
I'd told him this while he was living: how he climbed
that bird's leg like a vine. How bravely he carried
his sword in his teeth, and how his fists were full of feathers.

Conscription Papers

Here is the trouble with visiting the past:
it means dallying so long in the company of the dead.
And they brew their tea from such strange bark—
going down, it stings.

Hence my mother sends these tea-tan sheets
gone to powder in their creases.
Official business from the War Department:
You are now a soldier in the Army of the United States! Congratulations!

The irregular print of the 1940s
clots the windows of the *e*'s and *g*'s
where the metal arms swung from the typewriter well—
Cooperate by taking only small items which can be carried in your pockets.

Like a Saint Christopher medal to deflect the bullet.
Though the dead make good duffel bags for hunkering behind,
lugging them is a son of a bitch. So my mother
is a patriot, especially when she says, *Don't put me in your poem.*

His Soldier's Pay Record tells you what kind of people we are
because nothing is declared inside its little oaktag book
but his name, rank, and serial number, forget about
posterity—even my father's signature's in pencil.

At least war gives a man an afterlife as paperwork.
Somebody named S. J. Duboff witnessed its delivery.
Odds are, he's dead, so to mourn him I'll say: *Mr. Duboff,
may your soul be of the ilk that can embrace the accident of being here.*

. . .

And I know this is only a less-ochre echo of those other pages,
which I would tape here if they were not such frail
darkening scraps, about which my mother writes:
I don't want these so do with them what you will.

The Afterlife of the Fifties Dads

I wonder what they wear in heaven, they
    who mowed the lawn in the worn brown pants
        that once comprised one half
            of their good suits.

Have they lifted the wings
    from their wing-tipped shoes
        with the white spots where they'd gotten scuffed
        and which were given new life to mortify us

as we followed the lead of their pale legs,
    unsheathed when those pants were cut into shorts,
        exposing the ridiculous sockless Saturday ankles
        marching a beach chair across the beach?

And not until Saigon fell did their first jeans appear,
    a blue too flimsy, and the too-short bells
        pressed flat to flange both sides of their calves
        like the stiff fins of a flounder.

And when they finally broke down
    and bought discount sneakers,
        the strangely configured and wrong-colored stripes
        caused us to pretend that we did not know who they were.

But now I recognize their Florsheim shoes
    footprinting (like dance steps) the clouds overhead,
        in that Elysium where maybe they can finally throw a Frisbee
        without embarrassing themselves.

.   .   .

For they were good men: as proof, take the times
    we drove our jalopies dead-drunk into creeks
        and after we hiked home they sent us to the basement
        like raccoons disappearing down a storm grate.

Then through the floorboards we heard them clearly
    playing the part of the poor dumb schlub,
        telling the cops at the door they hadn't seen us, no—
        their sons, their daughters, wherever we were.

For the First Clone, Aging Now and Largely Forgotten

The sheep sleeps far away, in her paddock
in Scotland. All her dreaming is grass.
But I wonder if the other ever appears,
the one from whose cheek cell
she was made. Does she dream of a mother
with matronly dugs, or is her dream more
of a sister swiveling wildflowers in her cheek?
Or does her dream come with fur-dampening
night sweats: the test tube's wall, the world
visible, but bent. Or maybe she dreams
of a wolf's jiggling belly: all the *my what big* whatevers,
and she batted her way out with her hooves.
I'm thinking of Dolly Parton, her namesake:
the mass of white curls and the mass
of mascara—big eyes, big teeth, big nails, big teats
she never suckled from. Maybe this bodily surfeit
haunts her dreams. Sure, the gene sequence
tells us what we are, but so does what we lack.
As we humans think: I am part not who I am
but part someone else, the way it is
for all siblings of the missing halves,
like the plastic flip-flops floating up
on the beaches of Yucatán, never in pairs.
And picking one up I swear I could feel
the same thing I felt in the graveyard at Graceland
where Elvis lies planted beside his dead twin
by the kidney-shaped pool. And in the same way
the kidney pines for its twin, which is why
when I made a cake shaped like the gland
with the words *Bye Bye* spelled out in raisins
he who was slated for surgery started to sob

into the frosting's mauve-ish goo. Oops.
Plato's theory is that the egg's made of halves
separated at birth and which when united
will screw each other's brains out. I may
be taking liberties. Half of my husband
is pure radiant light while the other half
is a thundercloud with an anvil head—beats me
how the yolk and albumen can coexist.
And consider the ram in South Carolina
who knocked down an old couple and stomped them
to death. Fifty years married: I can't help but think
he was jealous of them, even though he's their pet,
because every day climbed the backs of their sheep
and he never found one who completed him.
It's not rape exactly, because who can say
what a sheep-woman wants: is he predacious?
Or does she desire him, the ram with his horns
so ornate they might be a costume, and he
is something other underneath? Now we're back
to the wolf who had no part in her making;
I know this with the sensible half of my brain.
But the other half says: as soon as she went into heat
the clone jumped the fence and took off with a ram,
who is much like a wolf in that both seem to need
one of the selective serotonin reuptake inhibitors
to calm the violent streak. Then, for the wolf,
a dye job and a perm. And is that really his fur
or just a dressing gown he wears? Looks good,
I must admit. Forgive my preoccupation
with the wolf and the ram: I've never cared much
for those who were one hundred percent sweet.
If it seems that I've all but forgotten the sheep—
can't help it. I have always been attracted
to the kind of men who were not made for me.

Night Festival, Olympia

Something about the parade I hated—
so much gaiety on a knife edge,
the captain of the samba band dressed up like a beast.
But hey, that's just me, the truculent me.
There is nothing inherently wrong with the idea
of humans being happy. As the thief says,
This will go easier if everyone cooperates.
So when a drunk stepped forward and asked for a quarter
I said, "How about a buck instead?"
with an exuberance rigged up to balance my mood:
I dug for the dollar, he stuck out his hand.
Then said, "I am a veteran," after I'd launched
my half of the shake, realizing then
the hand wasn't being offered: it was a proof.
As in: a mathematical summation.
He was showing me he had no fingers,
only two stubs whose taut raw skin
reflected pink tones with which the night glowed
as if we did not live in houses,
as if we huddled around the flames.
But this was in the parking lot at Safeway,
palace of the all-night goddess of cigs—
whose dull voltage lit my piety
when he held up his hand and I went ahead
with touching it, as if I were not afraid.

Eulogy from the Boardwalk Behind the KFC

Deschutes Parkway, 10/11/01

What is not part of the calamity goes on—
the salmon move upstream. Their colors
are borrowed from the heart of the water,
a camouflage blotchwork
of old bruises. They zigzag forth
in single file—tack left, tack right,
then pause and shiver, tack and shiver,
tack and shiver, tack and shatter—
when their shivering scatters
and leaves nothing at the core.
They get their discipline from the current
and go crazy in the calm—please notify
the human spectators: what is not part
goes crazy in the calm. The fish
are slightly darker than the water
whose feet we lay our shadows at—
all right, I know the water doesn't have feet
but how much precision do you expect
from us who stand here all strung out
on far-flung grief? At least I have tried
to describe the salmon honestly,
their knitted frenzy below the floodgate.
How we see them only if we look straight down
from this low bridge, where the cars scream past.
Straight down, and the water surface unsilvers;
what we see best are their white scars.

As Per the Geese:

So it's not their fault they void their bowels ninety times a day
and discharge as they waddle across the commons.
But we wish they'd manifest
at least some symptom of their shame,
instead of acting like we should be glad to have their green turds
for a gift. See how they swagger,
showing off their black necks, and the white strap
that makes them as mysterious as geishas.

Now no one dares spread out a picnic blanket
any day in the park, and who knows what we'll look like
when we are rendered entirely as dots?
See the young mothers
patrolling the lakeshore at dawn
the morning of the Easter egg hunt, with little shovels
and translucent grocery sacks that dangle from their wrists.
See how they squint like boxers, peering into the shaded mulch.

Oh these are not the people
we intended to become, back when we imagined ourselves
standing under parasols or our own ornate facial hair,
pushing prams or playing croquet on the lawn.
We each could be a sonnet, or a Chopin polonaise,
were we not so often sick at heart—
having felt the ground slide underneath us
as if the soil there had suddenly turned to grease.

. . .

Then naturally our thoughts turn to driving our big cars
straight into the heart of their adenoidal honks.
But instead we meekly hobble off, searching
for something solid against which to scrape our shoe.
Because we have to admit it's hard not to envy
the gumption it takes them to shit as they walk.
And not to look back at it, ever.
To not give a damn about being so unloved.

Salmon Song

For Scott Chambers

Let's not forget the fundamental processes
and from their wretchedness concoct a singing:

rot or scar, scar or rot—
either way we'll be made into something new.

Scar as the pale stripe born from blood,
a monument built by the broken skin

as the big fish noses its way upriver
with a snout crosshatched by each rough turn.

Versus rot, like the dead one snagged in the riffle
in the white flocking of its fungal suit

before the skin peels off like a opera glove, being spun
and flung by Rita Hayworth's *Gilda!*

On the one hand there's the sun-shrunk mummy
of the carcass perched on an alder stump

while the other hand's slick with spawned-out fish
souping the skids of the creek's thin thread.

Scar wins first but rot wins out,
singing its lullaby to the dregs,

its swan song to the scuttled forms:
oh thin white bones on the mud's brown bed.

Beauty Bark

The idea is, it makes life easier
by giving the unwanted thing
a looser hold. Never mind
how it comes in a fifty-pound sack—
the flowers must be suffered for.
So keep humping it to their beds on the far side of the lawn.

Whatever it is, it is not rotten yet:
this is death caught while it still looks good,
like the bird right after the window smack
or the corpse new in its casket—no odors,
no odors yet. Just a cedary smell,
never mind how the splinters make you itch.

See how the dead stuff chaperones the living,
with a brownness that makes the living look good
by not offering any competition,
like the buddy-girls of school.
You're supposed to overlook it
and not obsess on the jigsaw shapes,

not wonder where the beauty lies—
in the bark or in its other.
This isn't one of those dancer-or-the-dance type questions,
this isn't Yeats.
We all know what part of the tree it comes from:
oh substance eponymous.

.   .   .

But I wonder what you make of us
who grow crookedly out of the burial mulch:
us the brooded-by-death, the pricker-limbed, better get your
     leather gloves.
Good God, my thorns are sharp, and my root's so long
you can forget about screwdrivering it out.
But come August's wilt you will praise my random flower.

Shrike Tree

Most days back then I would walk by the shrike tree,
a dead hawthorn at the base of a hill.
The shrike had pinned smaller birds on the tree's black thorns
and the sun had stripped them of their feathers.

Some of the dead ones hung at eye level
while some burned holes in the sky overhead.
At least it is honest,
the body apparent
and not rotting in the dirt.

And I, having never seen the shrike at work,
can only imagine how the breasts were driven into the
    branches.
When I saw him he'd be watching from a different tree
with his mask like Zorro
and the gray cape of his wings.

At first glance he could have been a mockingbird or a jay
if you didn't take note of how his beak was hooked.
If you didn't know the ruthlessness of what he did—
ah, but that is a human judgment.

They are mute, of course, a silence at the center of a bigger
    silence,
these rawhide ornaments, their bald skulls showing.
And notice how I've slipped into the present tense
as if they were still with me.

Of course they are still with me.

．　．　．

They hang there, desiccating
by the trail where I walked, back when I could walk,
before life pinned me on its thorn.
It is ferocious, life, but it must eat,
then leaves us with the artifact.

Which is: these black silhouettes in the midday sun,
strict and jagged, like an Asian script.
A tragedy that is not without its glamour.
Not without the runes of the wizened meat.

Because imagine the luck!—to be plucked from the air,
to be drenched and dried in the sun's bright voltage—
well, hard luck is luck, nonetheless.
With a chunk of sky in each eye socket.
And the pierced heart strung up like a pearl.

Chum

How come we all don't have the luxury of our ghosts?
The way some paintings of salmon
show their spectral versions flying.
License, you might say,
for the artist to put dead fish in the sky.
Instead of leaving them as they are
when you see them wilting in the eddy:
two tons of major spent-sex stink.

Yet see how everyone skips so giddily around the trail—
eyeballing the spawning from this cedar bridge.
As if they're sure we will be cohorts
in the rapture about which the bumper stickers speak,
as if we really will ascend someday to swim among the fishes.
All of us: see how good we are,
so careful not to kick stones down into the creek.

I'm just trying to get a handle on how it would be
if we made love one time in our lives
(after days spent on the interstate)
before we lay down to die so publicly in shallow pools?
While the other forms pass by and point
to educate to their frenzied children:
See the odd species. They chose love.

Tapas

There are so many endings, served and again,
and only scant meat on the knucklebone.

But you and I, we will not let ourselves be daunted
by the prospect of tomorrow's stinking breath—

yes?

No, we say: Bring on the kisses inflected of squid
and let the dirty dishes click like castanets!

And let the starch on my tongue
be a good quarter-inch thick

when you—with your stout malformed fingers—push
the night's last olive through my lips.

ACKNOWLEDGMENTS

These poems first appeared in various forms in the following magazines: *American Poetry Review, Barrow Street, Bellingham Review, Black Warrior Review, Chicago Review, Crab Orchard Review, Indiana Review, The New Yorker, Northwest Review, The Paris Review, Pequod, River Styx, Solo, Swink, Sycamore Review, Third Coast, Triquarterly,* and *Western Humanities Review.* My thanks go to those who labor in what has become the obscure province—the tiny Liechtenstein—of paper, and to the people who buy these magazines.

The MacArthur Foundation and Southern Illinois University gave me the money, which translated into the time, to write these poems, and I am indebted.

Also I would like to thank the people who read my poems and gave their critical appraisals of various drafts: Bill Clegg, Roger Fanning, Rodney Jones, Tim Kelly, Mary Jane Knecht, Maria MacLeod, Jane Mead, Daniel Menaker, Jim Rudy, Ben Sonnenberg. Plus the other friends I'm sure I forgot.

About the Author

Lucia Perillo has published three previous collections: *The Oldest Map with the Name America; The Body Mutinies,* for which she won the PEN/Revson Foundation Poetry Fellowship and several other awards; and *Dangerous Life,* which received the Norma Farber Award from the Poetry Society of America. A 2000 MacArthur Fellow, her poems have appeared in such magazines as *The New Yorker, The Atlantic,* and *The Paris Review,* and they have been included in the Pushcart and Best American Poetry anthologies.

About the Type

This book is set in Spectrum, a typeface designed in the 1940s and the last from the distinguished Dutch type designer Jan van Krimpen. Spectrum is a polished and reserved font.